The Blooming LEADER

A WORKBOOK FOR ASPIRING LEADING LADIES

DR. DONISHIA YARDE

Table of Contents

Introduction

Welcome to "Blossoming into Leadership: A Workbook for Aspiring Leading Ladies!" This workbook is designed to guide you through a transformative journey of personal, spiritual, and business growth. By engaging with the exercises, reflections, and practices within these pages, you'll discover the tools and insights needed to blossom into the leader you aspire to be.

Overview

This workbook is divided into three main sections: Personal Growth, Spiritual Growth, and Business Growth. Each section contains exercises, questions, and action steps tailored to help you nurture various aspects of your life and leadership skills. Whether you're looking to enhance your self-awareness, deepen your spiritual connection, or cultivate entrepreneurial success, this workbook offers a comprehensive approach to holistic growth.

How to Use this Workbook

To get the most out of this workbook, take your time to engage with each exercise fully. Set aside dedicated moments for reflection, meditation, and action planning. Remember, this is a journey, not a race. Be patient with yourself and embrace the process of growth and self-discovery.

-Dr. Donishia Yarde

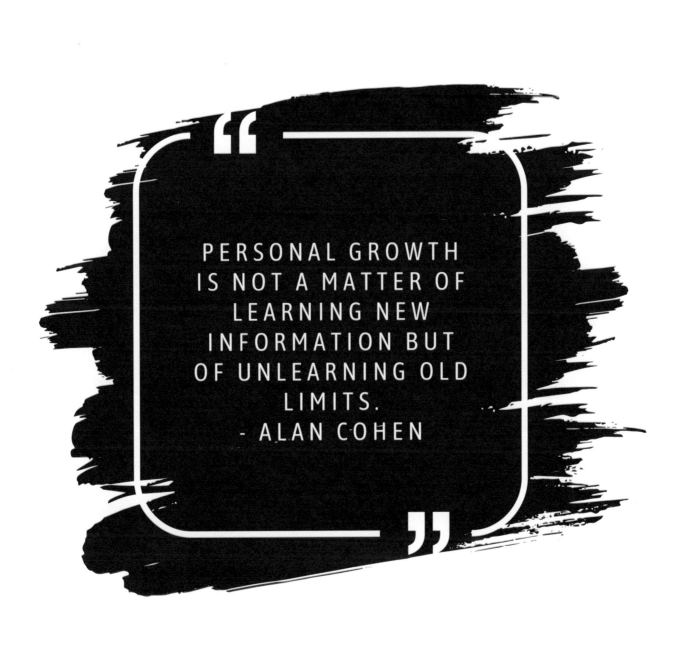

> PERSONAL GROWTH IS NOT A MATTER OF LEARNING NEW INFORMATION BUT OF UNLEARNING OLD LIMITS.
> - ALAN COHEN

SECTION 1:

Personal Growth

Personal growth is a lifelong journey of self-discovery, self-improvement, and self-actualization. It involves cultivating self-awareness, nurturing your well-being, and developing the skills and qualities that enable you to thrive in all areas of your life. In this section of the workbook, you'll embark on a transformative journey that will empower you to become the best version of yourself. Through a series of reflection prompts, exercises, and actionable strategies, you'll explore key aspects of personal growth, including self-reflection, self-care, confidence, and resilience.

Planting Seeds of Self-Reflection

Self-reflection is a powerful tool for personal growth and self-discovery. It allows you to pause, introspect, and gain deeper insights into your thoughts, feelings, and experiences. In this exercise, you'll engage with thought-provoking reflection prompts designed to help you explore who you are today and how your past experiences have shaped you.

By answering questions such as "Who Are You Today?" and "How have your experiences shaped the person you are today?", you'll gain valuable insights into your values, beliefs, strengths, and areas for growth. Additionally, the exercise of mapping your personal growth journey will enable you to identify patterns, milestones, and opportunities for development, empowering you to take proactive steps towards achieving your personal and professional goals.

Who Are You Today?

Use this space to uncover who you are and how you have transformed

Who Do You Desire To Be?

Use this space to describe the person you desire to be

Personal Progress Map

GOAL:					

START DATE: **DEADLINE:**

PROGRESS	10%	25%	50%	75%	100%

GOAL:					

START DATE: **DEADLINE:**

PROGRESS	10%	25%	50%	75%	100%

GOAL:					

START DATE: **DEADLINE:**

PROGRESS	10%	25%	50%	75%	100%

GOAL:					

START DATE: **DEADLINE:**

PROGRESS	10%	25%	50%	75%	100%

GOAL:					

START DATE: **DEADLINE:**

PROGRESS	10%	25%	50%	75%	100%

Personal Progress Map

GOAL:	

START DATE: **DEADLINE:**

PROGRESS	10%	25%	50%	75%	100%

GOAL:	

START DATE: **DEADLINE:**

PROGRESS	10%	25%	50%	75%	100%

GOAL:	

START DATE: **DEADLINE:**

PROGRESS	10%	25%	50%	75%	100%

GOAL:	

START DATE: **DEADLINE:**

PROGRESS	10%	25%	50%	75%	100%

GOAL:	

START DATE: **DEADLINE:**

PROGRESS	10%	25%	50%	75%	100%

Personal Progress Map

GOAL:					

START DATE: **DEADLINE:**

PROGRESS	10%	25%	50%	75%	100%

GOAL:					

START DATE: **DEADLINE:**

PROGRESS	10%	25%	50%	75%	100%

GOAL:					

START DATE: **DEADLINE:**

PROGRESS	10%	25%	50%	75%	100%

GOAL:					

START DATE: **DEADLINE:**

PROGRESS	10%	25%	50%	75%	100%

GOAL:					

START DATE: **DEADLINE:**

PROGRESS	10%	25%	50%	75%	100%

Personal Progress Map

GOAL:	

START DATE: **DEADLINE:**

PROGRESS	10%	25%	50%	75%	100%

GOAL:	

START DATE: **DEADLINE:**

PROGRESS	10%	25%	50%	75%	100%

GOAL:	

START DATE: **DEADLINE:**

PROGRESS	10%	25%	50%	75%	100%

GOAL:	

START DATE: **DEADLINE:**

PROGRESS	10%	25%	50%	75%	100%

GOAL:	

START DATE: **DEADLINE:**

PROGRESS	10%	25%	50%	75%	100%

Personal Progress Map

GOAL:	

START DATE: **DEADLINE:**

PROGRESS	10%	25%	50%	75%	100%

GOAL:	

START DATE: **DEADLINE:**

PROGRESS	10%	25%	50%	75%	100%

GOAL:	

START DATE: **DEADLINE:**

PROGRESS	10%	25%	50%	75%	100%

GOAL:	

START DATE: **DEADLINE:**

PROGRESS	10%	25%	50%	75%	100%

GOAL:	

START DATE: **DEADLINE:**

PROGRESS	10%	25%	50%	75%	100%

Nurturing Your Inner Garden

Self-care is an essential aspect of personal growth and well-being. It involves taking deliberate actions to nurture your mind, body, and soul, ensuring that you have the energy, resilience, and vitality to thrive in all areas of your life. In this section, you'll find a comprehensive self-care checklist categorized into mind, body, and soul. Explore daily rituals for self-love and identify practices that resonate with you, allowing you to create a personalized self-care routine that supports your overall well-being. By prioritizing self-care, you'll replenish your energy, reduce stress, and cultivate a strong foundation for personal growth and resilience.

Self-care manifests in various ways, all of which contribute positively to your overall well-being. Whether it's maintaining a consistent sleep routine, nourishing your body with healthy food, immersing yourself in nature, indulging in activities you love, or practicing gratitude, each form of self-care plays a vital role in enhancing your physical, emotional, and mental health.

Any action you take to prioritize your physical, mental, and emotional well-being constitutes self-care. Engaging in self-care not only enhances your overall health but also fosters improved physical vitality, mental clarity, and emotional balance.

Self-Care Checklist

DAILY BASIC/SOUL	M	T	W	T	F	S	S
WRITE GRATITUDE JOURNAL							
GET 8 HOURS SLEEP TONIGHT							
FORGIVE YOURSELF							
MEDITATE							
READ THE BIBLEK							
PAUSE & TAKE A DEEP BREATHE							

PHYSICAL/BODY	M	T	W	T	F	S	S
GO ON 30 MIN WALK DAILY							
DO A WORKOUT-EVEN IF ONLY 10 MINS							
HYDRATE-8 GLASS OF WATER							
COOK & EAT HEALTHY							
SOAK UP IN THE BATH WITH CANDLES							
STRETCH AFTER WORKING ON MY DESK							

WORK +BUSINESS/MIND	M	T	W	T	F	S	S
READ 10 PAGES OF BOOK							
LIMIT SOCIAL MEDIA							
TAKE A 5 MIN BREAK EVERY HOUR							
SET DAILY GOALS, TICK THEM OFF							
LEARN SOMETHING NEW							
LISTEN TO A PODCAST							

Self-Care Checklist

DAILY BASIC/SOUL	M	T	W	T	F	S	S
WRITE GRATITUDE JOURNAL							
GET 8 HOURS SLEEP TONIGHT							
FORGIVE YOURSELF							
MEDITATE							
READ THE BIBLEK							
PAUSE & TAKE A DEEP BREATHE							

PHYSICAL/BODY	M	T	W	T	F	S	S
GO ON 30 MIN WALK DAILY							
DO A WORKOUT-EVEN IF ONLY 10 MINS							
HYDRATE-8 GLASS OF WATER							
COOK & EAT HEALTHY							
SOAK UP IN THE BATH WITH CANDLES							
STRETCH AFTER WORKING ON MY DESK							

WORK +BUSINESS/MIND	M	T	W	T	F	S	S
READ 10 PAGES OF BOOK							
LIMIT SOCIAL MEDIA							
TAKE A 5 MIN BREAK EVERY HOUR							
SET DAILY GOALS, TICK THEM OFF							
LEARN SOMETHING NEW							
LISTEN TO A PODCAST							

Self-Care Checklist

DAILY BASIC/SOUL	M	T	W	T	F	S	S
WRITE GRATITUDE JOURNAL							
GET 8 HOURS SLEEP TONIGHT							
FORGIVE YOURSELF							
MEDITATE							
READ THE BIBLEK							
PAUSE & TAKE A DEEP BREATHE							

PHYSICAL/BODY	M	T	W	T	F	S	S
GO ON 30 MIN WALK DAILY							
DO A WORKOUT-EVEN IF ONLY 10 MINS							
HYDRATE-8 GLASS OF WATER							
COOK & EAT HEALTHY							
SOAK UP IN THE BATH WITH CANDLES							
STRETCH AFTER WORKING ON MY DESK							

WORK +BUSINESS/MIND	M	T	W	T	F	S	S
READ 10 PAGES OF BOOK							
LIMIT SOCIAL MEDIA							
TAKE A 5 MIN BREAK EVERY HOUR							
SET DAILY GOALS, TICK THEM OFF							
LEARN SOMETHING NEW							
LISTEN TO A PODCAST							

Self-Care Checklist

DAILY BASIC/SOUL	M	T	W	T	F	S	S
WRITE GRATITUDE JOURNAL							
GET 8 HOURS SLEEP TONIGHT							
FORGIVE YOURSELF							
MEDITATE							
READ THE BIBLEK							
PAUSE & TAKE A DEEP BREATHE							

PHYSICAL/BODY	M	T	W	T	F	S	S
GO ON 30 MIN WALK DAILY							
DO A WORKOUT-EVEN IF ONLY 10 MINS							
HYDRATE-8 GLASS OF WATER							
COOK & EAT HEALTHY							
SOAK UP IN THE BATH WITH CANDLES							
STRETCH AFTER WORKING ON MY DESK							

WORK +BUSINESS/MIND	M	T	W	T	F	S	S
READ 10 PAGES OF BOOK							
LIMIT SOCIAL MEDIA							
TAKE A 5 MIN BREAK EVERY HOUR							
SET DAILY GOALS, TICK THEM OFF							
LEARN SOMETHING NEW							
LISTEN TO A PODCAST							

Self-Care Checklist

DAILY BASIC/SOUL	M	T	W	T	F	S	S
WRITE GRATITUDE JOURNAL							
GET 8 HOURS SLEEP TONIGHT							
FORGIVE YOURSELF							
MEDITATE							
READ THE BIBLEK							
PAUSE & TAKE A DEEP BREATHE							

PHYSICAL/BODY	M	T	W	T	F	S	S
GO ON 30 MIN WALK DAILY							
DO A WORKOUT-EVEN IF ONLY 10 MINS							
HYDRATE-8 GLASS OF WATER							
COOK & EAT HEALTHY							
SOAK UP IN THE BATH WITH CANDLES							
STRETCH AFTER WORKING ON MY DESK							

WORK +BUSINESS/MIND	M	T	W	T	F	S	S
READ 10 PAGES OF BOOK							
LIMIT SOCIAL MEDIA							
TAKE A 5 MIN BREAK EVERY HOUR							
SET DAILY GOALS, TICK THEM OFF							
LEARN SOMETHING NEW							
LISTEN TO A PODCAST							

Self-Care Checklist

DAILY BASIC/SOUL	M	T	W	T	F	S	S
WRITE GRATITUDE JOURNAL							
GET 8 HOURS SLEEP TONIGHT							
FORGIVE YOURSELF							
MEDITATE							
READ THE BIBLEK							
PAUSE & TAKE A DEEP BREATHE							

PHYSICAL/BODY	M	T	W	T	F	S	S
GO ON 30 MIN WALK DAILY							
DO A WORKOUT-EVEN IF ONLY 10 MINS							
HYDRATE-8 GLASS OF WATER							
COOK & EAT HEALTHY							
SOAK UP IN THE BATH WITH CANDLES							
STRETCH AFTER WORKING ON MY DESK							

WORK +BUSINESS/MIND	M	T	W	T	F	S	S
READ 10 PAGES OF BOOK							
LIMIT SOCIAL MEDIA							
TAKE A 5 MIN BREAK EVERY HOUR							
SET DAILY GOALS, TICK THEM OFF							
LEARN SOMETHING NEW							
LISTEN TO A PODCAST							

Self-Care Checklist

DAILY BASIC/SOUL	M	T	W	T	F	S	S
WRITE GRATITUDE JOURNAL							
GET 8 HOURS SLEEP TONIGHT							
FORGIVE YOURSELF							
MEDITATE							
READ THE BIBLEK							
PAUSE & TAKE A DEEP BREATHE							

PHYSICAL/BODY	M	T	W	T	F	S	S
GO ON 30 MIN WALK DAILY							
DO A WORKOUT-EVEN IF ONLY 10 MINS							
HYDRATE-8 GLASS OF WATER							
COOK & EAT HEALTHY							
SOAK UP IN THE BATH WITH CANDLES							
STRETCH AFTER WORKING ON MY DESK							

WORK +BUSINESS/MIND	M	T	W	T	F	S	S
READ 10 PAGES OF BOOK							
LIMIT SOCIAL MEDIA							
TAKE A 5 MIN BREAK EVERY HOUR							
SET DAILY GOALS, TICK THEM OFF							
LEARN SOMETHING NEW							
LISTEN TO A PODCAST							

Self-Care Checklist

DAILY BASIC/SOUL	M	T	W	T	F	S	S
WRITE GRATITUDE JOURNAL							
GET 8 HOURS SLEEP TONIGHT							
FORGIVE YOURSELF							
MEDITATE							
READ THE BIBLEK							
PAUSE & TAKE A DEEP BREATHE							

PHYSICAL/BODY	M	T	W	T	F	S	S
GO ON 30 MIN WALK DAILY							
DO A WORKOUT-EVEN IF ONLY 10 MINS							
HYDRATE-8 GLASS OF WATER							
COOK & EAT HEALTHY							
SOAK UP IN THE BATH WITH CANDLES							
STRETCH AFTER WORKING ON MY DESK							

WORK +BUSINESS/MIND	M	T	W	T	F	S	S
READ 10 PAGES OF BOOK							
LIMIT SOCIAL MEDIA							
TAKE A 5 MIN BREAK EVERY HOUR							
SET DAILY GOALS, TICK THEM OFF							
LEARN SOMETHING NEW							
LISTEN TO A PODCAST							

Self-Care Checklist

DAILY BASIC/SOUL	M	T	W	T	F	S	S
WRITE GRATITUDE JOURNAL							
GET 8 HOURS SLEEP TONIGHT							
FORGIVE YOURSELF							
MEDITATE							
READ THE BIBLEK							
PAUSE & TAKE A DEEP BREATHE							

PHYSICAL/BODY	M	T	W	T	F	S	S
GO ON 30 MIN WALK DAILY							
DO A WORKOUT-EVEN IF ONLY 10 MINS							
HYDRATE-8 GLASS OF WATER							
COOK & EAT HEALTHY							
SOAK UP IN THE BATH WITH CANDLES							
STRETCH AFTER WORKING ON MY DESK							

WORK +BUSINESS/MIND	M	T	W	T	F	S	S
READ 10 PAGES OF BOOK							
LIMIT SOCIAL MEDIA							
TAKE A 5 MIN BREAK EVERY HOUR							
SET DAILY GOALS, TICK THEM OFF							
LEARN SOMETHING NEW							
LISTEN TO A PODCAST							

Self-Care Checklist

DAILY BASIC/SOUL	M	T	W	T	F	S	S
WRITE GRATITUDE JOURNAL							
GET 8 HOURS SLEEP TONIGHT							
FORGIVE YOURSELF							
MEDITATE							
READ THE BIBLEK							
PAUSE & TAKE A DEEP BREATHE							

PHYSICAL/BODY	M	T	W	T	F	S	S
GO ON 30 MIN WALK DAILY							
DO A WORKOUT-EVEN IF ONLY 10 MINS							
HYDRATE-8 GLASS OF WATER							
COOK & EAT HEALTHY							
SOAK UP IN THE BATH WITH CANDLES							
STRETCH AFTER WORKING ON MY DESK							

WORK +BUSINESS/MIND	M	T	W	T	F	S	S
READ 10 PAGES OF BOOK							
LIMIT SOCIAL MEDIA							
TAKE A 5 MIN BREAK EVERY HOUR							
SET DAILY GOALS, TICK THEM OFF							
LEARN SOMETHING NEW							
LISTEN TO A PODCAST							

Self-Care Checklist

DAILY BASIC/SOUL	M	T	W	T	F	S	S
WRITE GRATITUDE JOURNAL							
GET 8 HOURS SLEEP TONIGHT							
FORGIVE YOURSELF							
MEDITATE							
READ THE BIBLEK							
PAUSE & TAKE A DEEP BREATHE							

PHYSICAL/BODY	M	T	W	T	F	S	S
GO ON 30 MIN WALK DAILY							
DO A WORKOUT-EVEN IF ONLY 10 MINS							
HYDRATE-8 GLASS OF WATER							
COOK & EAT HEALTHY							
SOAK UP IN THE BATH WITH CANDLES							
STRETCH AFTER WORKING ON MY DESK							

WORK +BUSINESS/MIND	M	T	W	T	F	S	S
READ 10 PAGES OF BOOK							
LIMIT SOCIAL MEDIA							
TAKE A 5 MIN BREAK EVERY HOUR							
SET DAILY GOALS, TICK THEM OFF							
LEARN SOMETHING NEW							
LISTEN TO A PODCAST							

Cultivating Confidence and Resilience

Confidence and resilience are key qualities of effective leaders. They enable you to navigate life's ups and downs with grace, determination, and positivity, empowering you to overcome challenges and achieve your goals. In this section, you'll engage with the affirmation garden to grow positive self-talk and develop a deeper sense of self-belief.

Answer these questions "How can positive self-talk impact your confidence and resilience?" and creating an action plan for overcoming challenges below. You'll cultivate the mindset and skills needed to face adversity with courage and resilience.

Through reflection, exploration, and actionable strategies, you'll build the confidence and resilience required to lead with authenticity, compassion, and strength.

Self-talk Support

☐ Record your limiting beliefs & thoughts under inner critic

☐ Channel your inner coach by reframing each limiting statement

☐ Think about the words you would say to a loved one to instill courage

☐ Revisit your inner coach responses whenever you need support

Example: I can't do this   I give myself permission to try

INNER CRITIC

INNER COACH

"I grow through my mistakes"

Self-talk Support

- ☐ Record your limiting beliefs & thoughts under inner critic
- ☐ Channel your inner coach by reframing each limiting statement
- ☐ Think about the words you would say to a loved one to instill courage
- ☐ Revisit your inner coach responses whenever you need support

Example: I can't do this

I give myself permission to try

INNER CRITIC

INNER COACH

"I grow through my mistakes"

THE SOUL ALWAYS
KNOWS WHAT TO DO
TO HEAL ITSELF. THE
CHALLENGE IS TO
SILENCE THE MIND.
- CAROLINE MYSS

SECTION 2:

Spiritual Growth

Spiritual growth is a deeply personal and transformative journey that involves connecting with your inner spirit, exploring your beliefs and values, and seeking a deeper understanding of life's purpose and meaning. It transcends religious affiliations and dogmas, encompassing a broad spectrum of experiences and practices that nurture your soul and cultivate a sense of inner peace, harmony, and fulfillment. In this section of the workbook, you'll embark on a spiritual exploration that will empower you to connect with your inner essence, embrace gratitude and mindfulness, and discover your unique purpose and path in life.

BE STILL
and know that I am
GOD

Connecting with Your Inner Spirit

Connecting with your inner spirit is a foundational step in spiritual growth. It involves quieting the mind, tuning into your intuition, and cultivating a deeper awareness of your innermost thoughts, feelings, and desires. In this exercise, you'll engage in a guided exercises and meditation designed to help you find stillness within and connect with your inner spirit. You'll gain valuable insights into what truly matters to you and how you can align your actions with your core principles.

Checking In

How has my relationship with God grown or changed recently?

_____

_____

_____

What are some areas of my faith journey that I would like to focus on?

_____

_____

_____

Ways I am seeing God's love and presence in my life:

_____

_____

_____

Challenges and struggles I am facing in my faith journey:

_____

_____

_____

My blessings and answered prayers that have deepened my trust in God's faithfulness:

_____

_____

_____

Recent lessons from the scripture that have impacted me and provided guidance in my life:

_____

_____

_____

Write a letter to God expressing your hopes, dreams, worries and fears. Share your heart openly and honestly.

✝

God is my refuge

Embracing Gratitude and Mindfulness

Gratitude and mindfulness are powerful practices that can enrich your daily life and deepen your spiritual connection. Gratitude cultivates a sense of appreciation for the blessings and opportunities in your life, while mindfulness fosters a present-moment awareness that allows you to navigate everyday challenges with grace and ease. In this section, you'll explore the power of cultivating thankfulness through the gratitude garden and learn practical mindfulness techniques that can help you stay grounded, centered, and focused on what truly matters. Let's start by answering "In what ways can practicing gratitude enhance your daily life?" and "How can mindfulness help you navigate everyday challenges?"

Gratitude

Take a moment to reflect on the blessings in your life. Write down all of the things you are thankful for and reflect on God's faithfulness.

BLESSED AND GRATEFUL

grateful heart
Thankful soul

Seeking Purpose and Fulfillment

Aligning your actions with your values and purpose is essential for living a fulfilling and meaningful life. In this exercise, you'll complete a purpose discovery worksheet designed to help you clarify your core values, identify your passions and strengths, and articulate your unique purpose and vision for your life. Whether you're navigating a career transition, diving into a new creative pursuit, or aiming to create positive change within your community, aligning your actions with your values will empower you to lead a life that is genuine, purpose-driven, and deeply fulfilling.

Reflect on Values:

- Take a few moments to reflect on your core values. Consider what principles and beliefs are most important to you. Write down three to five values that resonate deeply with you.

Identify Actions:

- Think about your daily actions and choices in various areas of your life, such as career, relationships, and personal development. Identify actions that align with each of your core values. For example, if one of your core values is "compassion," you might identify actions like volunteering, active listening, or supporting a friend in need.

Seeking Purpose and Fulfillment

Reflect on Alignment:

Reflect on the following questions:

- How does aligning your actions with your values contribute to a richer, more purposeful life?

- In what ways can you ensure that your choices and actions reflect your core beliefs and contribute to your overall well-being and success?

Create Action Steps:

- Based on your reflections, create actionable steps to ensure that your choices and actions align with your core values. For each action step, specify what you will do, when you will do it, and how it aligns with your values.

Goal Setting

START DATE

DEADLINE

GOAL STATEMENT

WHY

- _____
- _____
- _____
- _____
- _____
- _____

ACTION PLAN

WHAT

- _____
- _____
- _____
- _____
- _____

Goal Setting

START DATE

DEADLINE

GOAL STATEMENT

ACTION PLAN

WHY

- [ ] _____
- [ ] _____
- [ ] _____
- [ ] _____
- [ ] _____
- [ ] _____

WHAT

- [ ] _____
- [ ] _____
- [ ] _____
- [ ] _____
- [ ] _____

Goal Setting

START DATE

DEADLINE

GOAL STATEMENT

WHY

- ▪ _____
- ▪ _____
- ▪ _____
- ▪ _____
- ▪ _____
- ▪ _____

ACTION PLAN

WHAT

- ▪ _____
- ▪ _____
- ▪ _____
- ▪ _____
- ▪ _____

Goal Setting

START DATE	DEADLINE

GOAL STATEMENT

WHY

- _____
- _____
- _____
- _____
- _____
- _____

ACTION PLAN

WHAT

- _____
- _____
- _____
- _____
- _____

Goal Setting

START DATE

DEADLINE

GOAL STATEMENT

ACTION PLAN

WHY

- ■ ____________________
- ■ ____________________
- ■ ____________________
- ■ ____________________
- ■ ____________________
- ■ ____________________

WHAT

- ■ ____________________
- ■ ____________________
- ■ ____________________
- ■ ____________________
- ■ ____________________

Goal Setting

START DATE

DEADLINE

GOAL STATEMENT

ACTION PLAN

WHY

- _____
- _____
- _____
- _____
- _____
- _____

WHAT

- _____
- _____
- _____
- _____
- _____

Goal Setting

START DATE

DEADLINE

GOAL STATEMENT

WHY

- ☐ _____
- ☐ _____
- ☐ _____
- ☐ _____
- ☐ _____
- ☐ _____

ACTION PLAN

WHAT

- ☐ _____
- ☐ _____
- ☐ _____
- ☐ _____
- ☐ _____

Goal Setting

START DATE

DEADLINE

GOAL STATEMENT

ACTION PLAN

WHY

- _____
- _____
- _____
- _____
- _____
- _____

WHAT

- _____
- _____
- _____
- _____
- _____

Goal Setting

START DATE

DEADLINE

GOAL STATEMENT

WHY

- _____
- _____
- _____
- _____
- _____
- _____

ACTION PLAN

WHAT

- _____
- _____
- _____
- _____
- _____

Goal Setting

START DATE

DEADLINE

GOAL STATEMENT

ACTION PLAN

WHY

- _____
- _____
- _____
- _____
- _____
- _____

WHAT

- _____
- _____
- _____
- _____
- _____

SECTION 3:

Business Growth

Business growth is a dynamic and multifaceted journey that involves cultivating entrepreneurial skills, fostering innovation, and building strong leadership and teamwork capabilities. It encompasses a range of activities and strategies aimed at expanding your business, increasing profitability, and creating sustainable value for your customers, employees, and stakeholders. In this section of the workbook, you'll explore key aspects of business growth, including entrepreneurship, vision planning, innovation, and leadership development. Through a series of exercises, reflection prompts, and actionable strategies, you'll gain insights and tools to propel your business forward, optimize performance, and achieve your growth objectives.

What Does A Successful Business Look Like for You?

Vision Board

CAREER	FINANCE

FRIENDS	LOVE

PERSONAL GROWTH	HEALTH

LEISURE	HOME

Planting the Seeds of Entrepreneurship

Entrepreneurship is the foundation of business growth. It involves identifying opportunities, taking calculated risks, and executing strategic plans to create and grow a successful business. In this exercise, you'll engage in a vision board exercise designed to help you visualize your business goals and aspirations.

Why is visualizing your business goals important for entrepreneurial success?" and creating an action step to outline your business objectives, target market, and growth strategies, you'll lay the groundwork for a thriving and sustainable business. Whether you're launching a new venture or scaling an existing business, cultivating an entrepreneurial mindset and strategic planning are essential for driving growth and achieving long-term success.

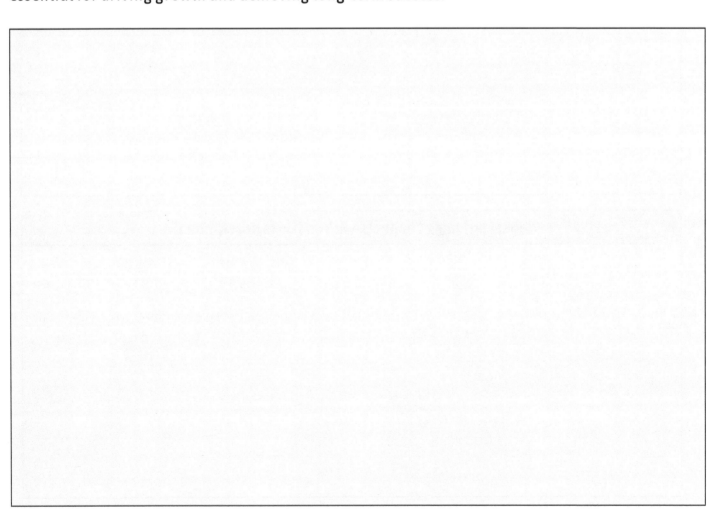

Business Plan

Your Business Product or Services

What Problem Does it Solve?

Who is Your Ideal Client

What Marketing Channels will You Use to Reach Them?

Your Business Product or Services

What Problem Does it Solve?

Who is Your Ideal Client

What Marketing Channels will You Use to Reach Them?

Business Plan

Your Business Product or Services

What Problem Does it Solve?

Who is Your Ideal Client

What Marketing Channels will You Use to Reach Them?

Business Plan

Your Business Product or Services

What Problem Does it Solve?

Who is Your Ideal Client

What Marketing Channels will You Use to Reach Them?

Business Plan

Your Business Product or Services

What Problem Does it Solve?

Who is Your Ideal Client

What Marketing Channels will You Use to Reach Them?

Embracing Innovation and Adaptability

In today's rapidly evolving business landscape, innovation and adaptability are crucial for staying competitive and seizing new opportunities. In this section, you'll explore strategies for fostering innovation within your business and learn how to adapt to changes effectively to stay ahead of the curve. By reflecting on questions such as "How can fostering a culture of innovation contribute to business growth?" and "What strategies can you implement to adapt to changing market conditions?", you'll discover how innovation and adaptability can drive business growth, enhance customer satisfaction, and create a sustainable competitive advantage. Whether it's introducing new products or services, adopting new technologies, or refining your business processes, embracing innovation and adaptability are key to unlocking new growth opportunities and ensuring long-term business success.

Innovation Map

Client Needs

Ideas to Solve Them

Date of Action	Tasks: How will you implement the idea?	DONE
		☐
		☐
		☐
		☐
		☐
		☐
		☐
		☐
		☐
		☐
		☐
		☐
		☐

Innovation Map

Client Needs	Ideas to Solve Them

Date of Action	Tasks: How will you implement the idea?	DONE
_____	_____	☐
_____	_____	☐
_____	_____	☐
_____	_____	☐
_____	_____	☐
_____	_____	☐
_____	_____	☐
_____	_____	☐
_____	_____	☐
_____	_____	☐
_____	_____	☐
_____	_____	☐
_____	_____	☐
_____	_____	☐

Innovation Map

Client Needs	Ideas to Solve Them

Date of Action	Tasks: How will you implement the idea?	DONE
_____	_____	☐
_____	_____	☐
_____	_____	☐
_____	_____	☐
_____	_____	☐
_____	_____	☐
_____	_____	☐
_____	_____	☐
_____	_____	☐
_____	_____	☐
_____	_____	☐
_____	_____	☐
_____	_____	☐

Innovation Map

Client Needs

Ideas to Solve Them

Date of Action	Tasks: How will you implement the idea?	DONE
_____	_____	☐
_____	_____	☐
_____	_____	☐
_____	_____	☐
_____	_____	☐
_____	_____	☐
_____	_____	☐
_____	_____	☐
_____	_____	☐
_____	_____	☐
_____	_____	☐
_____	_____	☐
_____	_____	☐
_____	_____	☐

Innovation Map

Client Needs	Ideas to Solve Them

Date of Action	Tasks: How will you implement the idea?	DONE
_____	_____	☐
_____	_____	☐
_____	_____	☐
_____	_____	☐
_____	_____	☐
_____	_____	☐
_____	_____	☐
_____	_____	☐
_____	_____	☐
_____	_____	☐
_____	_____	☐
_____	_____	☐
_____	_____	☐

Cultivating Leadership and Teamwork

Effective leadership and teamwork are essential for fostering a positive work environment, driving employee engagement, and achieving business growth. In this exercise, you'll develop your leadership skills through practical exercises and learn how to build and lead high-performing teams that contribute to the success of your business. By reflecting on questions such as "What qualities make a great leader?" and "How can effective teamwork contribute to achieving business objectives?", you'll gain insights into the importance of leadership and teamwork in driving business growth and creating a culture of collaboration and excellence. Whether you're leading a small team or managing a large organization, cultivating leadership skills and promoting teamwork are essential for maximizing productivity, fostering innovation, and achieving your business growth goals.

Build Your Team

Define Clear Roles and Responsibilities

_____

_____

_____

_____

_____

Who is on your team?

Who Do You Need to Hire?

How Do You Foster Open Communication

How Do You Promote Teamwork

Build Your Team

How can you be a better leader?

_____

_____

_____

_____

_____

Opportunities for Growth and Development

Evaluate and Adjust

Ways You Recognize and Reward Performance

Celebrate Wins

"
SUCCESS
USUALLY COMES
TO THOSE WHO
ARE TOO BUSY
TO BE LOOKING
FOR IT.
- HENRY DAVID
THOREAU
"

CONCLUSION

You Did It!

As you reach the end of "Blossoming into Leadership: A Workbook for Aspiring Leading Ladies," it's important to reflect on the transformative journey you've embarked upon. This workbook was designed to empower you to cultivate personal growth, spiritual enlightenment, and business acumen, equipping you with the tools, insights, and strategies needed to blossom into the leader you aspire to be.

Throughout this workbook, you've explored the depths of self-reflection, nurturing your inner garden, cultivating confidence and resilience, connecting with your inner spirit, embracing gratitude and mindfulness, seeking purpose and fulfillment, planting the seeds of entrepreneurship, embracing innovation and adaptability, and cultivating leadership and teamwork. Each section was carefully crafted to guide you through a holistic journey of self-discovery, personal development, and professional growth.

Remember, personal growth is a continuous journey of learning, evolving, and becoming. It requires commitment, dedication, and a willingness to step outside your comfort zone to embrace new challenges, opportunities, and experiences. Spiritual growth invites you to connect with your inner essence, explore your beliefs and values, and seek a deeper understanding of life's purpose and meaning. Business growth challenges you to innovate, adapt, and lead with vision, resilience, and integrity, fostering a culture of collaboration, excellence, and success.

CONCLUSION

You Did It!

As you move forward on your journey, I encourage you to embrace the lessons learned, celebrate your achievements, and continue to invest in your personal, spiritual, and professional growth. Surround yourself with positive influences, seek mentorship and guidance, and never stop learning, growing, and striving for excellence in all areas of your life.

Thank you for allowing "Blossoming into Leadership: A Workbook for Aspiring Leading Ladies" to be a part of your journey towards becoming the best version of yourself. May you continue to blossom, thrive, and inspire others with your unique gifts, talents, and leadership qualities.

Wishing you continued success, fulfillment, and joy on your path to leadership and personal mastery.

-Dr. Donishia Yarde

Journal

Journal

Journal

Journal

Journal

Journal

Journal

Journal

Journal

Journal

Journal

Journal

Journal

Journal

Journal

Journal

Journal

Journal

Journal

Journal

Journal

Journal

Journal

Journal

Journal

Journal

Journal

Made in the USA
Columbia, SC
26 April 2024

34744818R00058